BABY'S FAVORITE RHYMES TO SIGN

Sing and Sign the Classics
with Your Baby . . .
Before Your Baby Can Talk!

THREE RIVERS PRESS • NEW YORK

BABY'S FAVORITE RHYMES TO SIGN

Penny Warner • Illustrated by Gilbert Ford

Library of Congress Cataloging-in-Publication Data

Warner, Penny.
Baby's favorite rhymes to sign / Penny Warner;
Illustrated by Gilbert Ford.—1st ed.
p. cm.
Includes index.
1. American Sign Language.   2. Nursery rhymes.
3. Nonverbal communication in infants.
4. Sign language acquisition.   I. Title.
HV2476.4.W37 2010
419'.7—dc22   2010000575

ISBN 978-0-307-46043-1

Printed in the United States of America

Design by Maria Elias

10 9 8 7 6 5 4 3 2 1

First Edition

To Bradley, Luke, Stephanie, and Lyla,
the next generation of signers —PW

To all the New York subway passengers who inspired
the characters drawn in this book —GF

Also by Penny Warner

Rock-a-Bye Baby: 200 Ways to Get Baby to Sleep

Smart Start for Your Baby

Baby Play and Learn

Preschool Play and Learn

365 Toddler Tips

365 Baby Care Tips

Quality Time Anytime

Summer Smarts for Cool Kids

Learn to Sign the Fun Way!

Signing Fun

Great Games for Kids on the Go

Baby Birthday Parties

Illustrated and written by Gilbert Ford

Flying Lessons

CONTENTS

PREFACE

American Sign Language (ASL) has fascinated me since I learned the manual alphabet in sixth grade. My teacher, Neil Christiansen, was an innovative and creative instructor who made learning fun. He knew that teaching his class how to finger spell and sign would get us excited about playing with language. I'll bet he never dreamed that one day I'd become a sign language teacher as a result of this vividly visual experience.

Growing up, I taught many friends how to finger spell and sign—mainly so we could "talk" in secret behind our teachers' backs. As my skills improved, so did my interests in American Sign Language and Deaf Culture. I began taking courses in both ASL (a unique language used by American deaf people with its own vocabulary and syntax) and in SEE sign (Seeing Exact English, where each word of English has a corresponding sign). My ASL teacher, Beverly Wilson, took me under her wing and introduced me to the local Deaf Community, where I practiced my signs while getting to know many wonderful deaf people. When Beverly retired, she offered me the responsibility of teaching her sign class—and started me on a path toward getting my master's degree in Special Education/Deafness at San Francisco State University.

There, under the tutelage of Dr. Eileen Jackson and Dr. Arthurlene Turner, I learned how to teach language skills to deaf children while improving my own signing skills. After acquiring my degrees, I landed my first job: teaching deaf infants, toddlers, and preschoolers at Gregory Gardens School in Pleasant Hill, California. What an exhilarating experience it was to see these very young students learn to communicate through American Sign Language!

Signing had become an essential part of my everyday life. I went on to teach ASL and special education courses at Chabot Community College, and eventually began writing sign language books for kids—and even a mystery series featuring a deaf woman who solves crimes in the California Gold Country (*Dead Body Language* won a Macavity Award for Best First Mystery). While teaching, I noticed there were plenty of sign books for adults on the market, but very few for children. I'd fallen in love with sign language as a child, and I knew how much signing could improve children's language, spelling, and cognitive skills in a fun way, even from a very young age. That inspired me to write *Learn to Sign the Fun Way!* and *Signing Fun* specifically for children.

Here, with my new book, *Baby's Favorite Rhymes to Sign*, I've come full circle. After learning sign language as a child, it was only natural that I teach my own children sign language as they grew up. Now that they have children of their own, I have the opportunity to teach my grandbabies, Bradley, Luke, Stephanie, and Baby Girl Melvin, how to sign as well! And what better way to learn than to incorporate their favorite nursery rhymes and songs into sign language, making it easier for both parent and baby to learn this exciting and beautiful form of communication!

My grandson Luke signing "more."

(Photo by Kelli Nicole Saunders)

INTRODUCTION

The enthusiasm for teaching babies sign language is astounding! Baby sign books line the parenting shelves, and baby sign classes have become extremely popular. That's because parents now know that teaching their babies sign language helps little ones establish communication even before they can talk. This visual language helps babies develop basic vocabulary, as well as receptive and expressive language skills. Signing can lessen a baby's frustration with trying to express him- or herself, and parents are now able to help their young children communicate with their hands before they speak their first words!

In addition, it's been documented that babies who sign eventually have better verbal and cognitive skills than non-signers. According to a study published in 2000 by BabySigns.com, babies who learn to sign are not only better able to communicate their needs, but they're also more advanced in their language skills. Thanks to signing, babies have already begun to give meaning to words, and once they start to talk, their vocalized vocabulary grows quickly.

While there are plenty of beginning baby sign books available, what we need now are more baby sign language books that *continue to* develop those new and crucial skills in a fun way. *Baby's Favorite Rhymes to Sign* was written as an adjunct to the many basic vocabulary-based baby sign books on the market. But instead of teaching signs in a dictionary format, *Baby's Favorite Rhymes to Sign* helps you teach your baby to use ASL in a familiar context, through popular nursery rhymes.

Using well-loved, recognizable songs and rhymes is the best way to learn sign language for *both* you and your child. Instead of having to learn all new lyrics, which takes time, you already know the words. Furthermore, your baby has most likely heard these popular songs, too, but when sign is added, they come alive, visually and cognitively.

As a longtime American Sign Language teacher and the author of the best-selling book *Learn to Sign the Fun Way!*, I created *Baby's Favorite Rhymes to Sign* for parents to use with their baby to reinforce signing while enjoying time spent together. This new and unique sign book offers parents the opportunity to easily add signs to favorite, familiar songs, such as "Twinkle, Twinkle Little Star" and "Rock-a-Bye Baby," while building their young children's vocabulary, strengthening their command of ASL, and most of all offering a fun bonding experience. And sign is easy to incorporate throughout your baby's day. You can sign while feeding your baby, playing with her, changing her, bathing her, or even doing your chores within her view.

Inside *Baby's Favorite Rhymes to Sign*, you'll find:

- Many of the common, basic signs used in ASL, which will reinforce any signs you've already learned, plus additional signs to expand your vocabulary.
- Helpful tips on how to sign (i.e., how to hold your hand, how to do the movements, etc.) and how to "sing" in sign, rather than just "talk."
- Chapters divided into similarly themed rhymes and songs for easy reference and use.
- Whimsical illustrations of each sign, which make the book appealing for the parent as well as the baby.

The Basics of ASL

You might be surprised to learn that American Sign Language is the fourth most common language used in the United States. It's become so popular that children of all ages are learning basic finger spelling and signs, and older kids are taking classes at the high school and college levels as their foreign language option. Most signs are not difficult to learn. Many even resemble natural gestures, such as "banana" ("peeling" your index finger like a banana) and "baby" (rocking your arms as if cradling a baby).

ASL is recognized as a distinct language of its own, not a shortcut version of English. Although ASL has its own syntax and grammar, the structure of the sentences generally makes sense and is easy to translate. The first word in the sentence is usually the most important word, followed by the next, and so on, while unnecessary words are omitted. For example, if you want to say, "I am going to the store," you might sign, "Me store go" or "Store me go."

Using sign with a baby seems natural, since most parents simplify their sentences when talking to their babies. Instead of saying, "Baby, how would you like a bottle of milk right now?" we generally say something like, "Baby want milk?" The same is true of ASL, making it even easier for babies to learn. When you sing and sign the rhymes in *Baby's Favorite Rhymes to Sign*, you'll find excess words omitted, not only to make signing easier for you, but also to make it easier for your baby to follow. Furthermore, you'll enjoy the beauty of signing as you flow from one sign to the next.

Finally, the signs provided in *Baby's Favorite Rhymes to Sign* are described in detail and illustrated so they're clear and easy to perform. The following tips will also help you to make signs correctly.

Helpful Signing Tips

Just like speaking clearly to be understood, you need to learn how to sign clearly so your baby can begin to learn the signs. Here are some basic tips on how to sign with your baby.

- Use your dominant hand when signing, unless instructed otherwise. When two hands are involved in a sign, a reference to the right and/or left hand is included. (Left-handers will reverse these.)

- When signing a word or a letter, hold your hand palm out, so your baby can see the sign.

- When moving from one sign to another, keep your hand steady and your movements smooth. Don't bounce your hand or move it needlessly.

- Sign slowly for your baby, and keep the words and songs simple. You don't need to sign every word. (ASL signers often omit unnecessary words, such as "the" or "am.")

- As you sign, be sure to speak the words or sing the lyrics, so your baby can associate the spoken word with the sign.

- Use facial expressions and body language when you sign to help express the word or concept. For example, if you sign the word "happy," smile and look happy!

- If an object you're talking about is nearby, you can simply point to it. If you're talking about an object that's not visible, sign the word first, then point to the side, as if pointing to the object. The next time you point to the same spot, it will be understood that you are referencing the object you indicated.

- Signs that have to do with males, such as "boy," "father," and "man," are generally signed near the forehead. Signs for females, such as "girl," "mother," and "woman," are generally signed near the chin.

When singing and signing a nursery rhyme, move gracefully from one sign to the next. It takes practice, but that's what makes signing so beautiful. And your baby will love watching your dancing fingers and hands!

Seven Basic Hand Shapes

Most signs use seven basic hand shapes. Practice these a few times and you'll be ready to sign your first song!

Flat O  shape your hand like an O, but flattened a little

Flat hand  keep your hand flat, fingers together

Open hand  spread your fingers (this is also the sign for the number 5)

Bent hand

bend your hand
at a 45-degree angle

Curved hand

make a cupped hand

Closed hand or fist

make a fist

Claw hand

hold your hand like a claw,
fingers bent and spread apart

Name Signs

Many deaf people have "name signs"—a sign that incorporates the first letter of the person's name with either his or her gender or a physical characteristic. That way they don't have to finger spell their name each time it's used. They simply use the name sign as a shortcut. You may want to give your baby a name sign so you don't have to spell the letters of his or her name each time you include it in a rhyme or song. Here are some suggestions for name signs:

- Use the first initial of your baby's name and tap it in the "boy" or "girl" area of the head. (See page 4.)
- Select one of your baby's traits, such as her curly hair or his freckles, and use your baby's first initial as you gesture the trait. For example, you might make small circles near your face for curls or tap on your face for freckles.

If your baby's name already has a sign, such as "Rose," use that sign (the letter R tapped on either side of your nose).

How to Use This Book

Relax. You don't need any previous experience with ASL to learn the signs in the book. We've kept the rhymes simple, for both you and your baby, and provided fun illustrations and clear descriptions for each sign. The book is divided into logical parts, beginning with the "Alphabet Song," so you can learn the basic letters of the manual alphabet first. Part Two offers rhymes with concrete vocabulary words your baby may already be familiar with, such as the animals in "Old MacDonald Had a Farm." You'll find more active rhymes in Part Three, rhymes that incorporate a lot of verbs, such as "If You're Happy and You Know It." Part Four is full of surprises to keep your baby's attention, like "Pat-a-Cake" and "Where Is Thumbkin?" We wind down in Part Five with bedtime rhymes, such as "Rock-a-Bye Baby." And finally, Part Six includes your favorite rhymes and songs for special occasions, such as "Happy Birthday."

At the end of the book you'll find resources for more sign books, videos, and games, including my best-selling book for children, *Learn to Sign the Fun Way!* By the way, you don't have to follow the format—feel free to jump around to your favorite rhymes. Each sign is represented, even if it's repeated, so you don't have to learn one song before going on to the next.

Now let's get started singing and signing nursery rhymes to your baby!

ABCs

and

123s

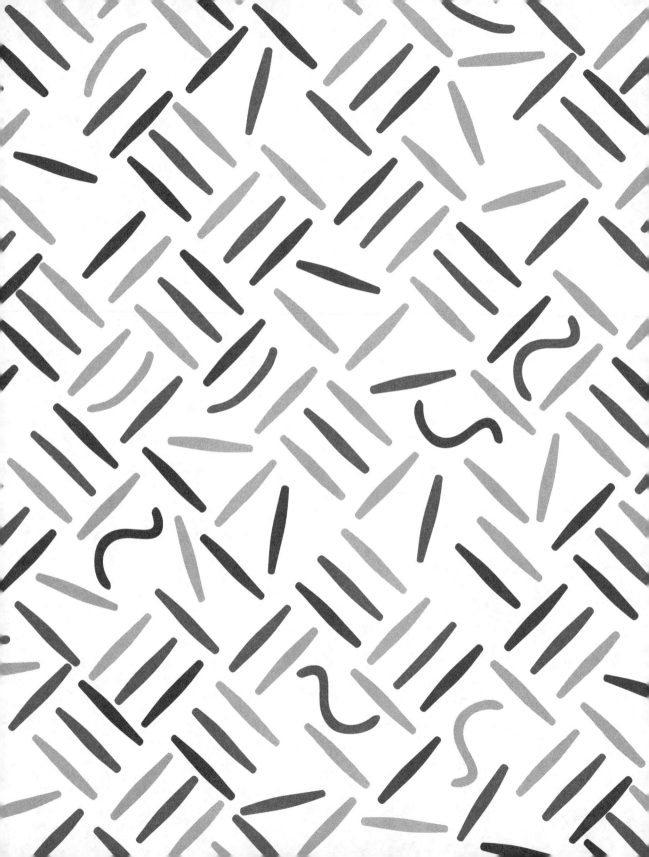

ALPHABET SONG

 A  Hold up fist, with thumb to the side

 B  Hold up flat hand, with thumb in middle of palm

C  Shape C with fingers and thumb

D  Shape D, with index finger extended, other fingers and thumb touching

E  Bend fingers; place bent thumb under fingertips

F  Touch tip of index finger to tip of thumb; extend remaining fingers

G,  Extend index finger and thumb, with remaining fingers tucked in, as if in a fist

H

Extend index and middle fingers, with remaining fingers and thumb tucked in, as if in a fist

I

Extend pinky finger; tuck in remaining fingers and thumb

J

Draw J with pinky finger; keep remaining fingers and thumb tucked in

K

Extend index and middle fingers, place thumb tip against middle finger, and tuck in remaining fingers

L  Shape L with index finger and thumb; tuck in remaining fingers

M  Fold index, middle, and ring fingers over thumb; tuck in pinky finger

N  Fold index and middle fingers over thumb; tuck in remaining fingers

O  Shape O with fingers and thumb

P,  Make the same shape as K, but turned, with index and middle fingers facing down

Q  Make the same shape as G, but turned, with thumb and index finger pointing down

R  Cross index and middle fingers and tuck in remaining fingers

S,  Make a fist, with thumb across fingers

T

Tuck thumb between index and middle fingers; tuck in remaining fingers

U

Hold up index and middle fingers, touching; tuck in remaining fingers

V,

Shape V with index and middle fingers; tuck in remaining fingers

W

Shape W with index, middle, and ring fingers; tuck in thumb and pinky finger

X,  Crook index finger; tuck in remaining fingers

Y  Extend thumb and pinky finger; tuck in remaining fingers

and  Move open hand left to right across chest, changing to a flat O

Z.  Draw Z with index finger; tuck in remaining fingers

Now  Cup hands, palms up, then move them down

I  Point to chest

know  Place fingertips of open hand on forehead

my  Place flat hand on chest

A  Hold up fist, with thumb to the side

B  Hold up flat hand, with thumb in middle of palm

C(**'s**).  Shape C with fingers and thumb

Next  Place flat right hand behind flat left hand, then move it up, over, and in front of left hand

time

Tap back of left wrist with right index finger

won't

[will]

Move flat hand forward from side of head

you

Point to baby

sing

Place U at mouth, then move it outward, waving the U up and down (as if sound waves are coming from your mouth)

with

Place A's together, palms facing each other

me?

Point to chest

ONE, TWO, BUCKLE MY SHOE

One,  Hold up index finger

two,  Hold up index and middle fingers

buckle  Interlink index fingers and thumbs of both hands

my  Place flat hand on chest

shoe.  Tap S's, facedown, together twice

Three,  Hold up thumb and index and middle fingers

four,  Hold up four fingers

shut

Place sides of flat hands together, palms out, as if shutting doors

(the) **door.**

Open and close right hand next to left hand

Five,

Hold up five fingers

six,

Touch tip of thumb to tip of pinky finger, with remaining fingers extended

pick up  Lift up right hand, palm down, and connect thumb and index finger as if picking something up

sticks.  Place right G on top of left G; raise right G up to shape stick

Seven,  Touch tip of thumb to tip of ring finger, with remaining fingers extended

eight,  Touch tip of thumb to tip of middle finger, with remaining fingers extended

lay

Lay faceup right V on left palm

them

Point to an imaginary "them," moving index finger from center to right

straight.

Hold side of B in front of face; move it forward, as if directing straight ahead

Nine,

Touch tip of thumb to tip of index finger, with remaining fingers extended

ten,  Point thumb of A up; wiggle hand side to side

do  Make claw hands, facedown; move side to side simultaneously

(it) **again!**  Cup right hand, palm up, then flip it over so right fingertips land in left palm

THIS OLD MAN

This  Point to an imaginary person (or man)

old  Zigzag S down from chin, like a long, wavy beard

man,  Move thumb of 5 from forehead to chest

he  Point to imaginary man

played  Twist Y's back and forth

one.  Hold up index finger

He  Point to imaginary man

played  Twist Y's back and forth

knick-knack  Knock twice

on  Place flat right palm on back of flat left hand

my  Place flat hand on chest

thumb.

Hold up thumb and wiggle it

(With a)
**knick-
knack,**

Knock twice

**paddy
whack,**

Knock twice with other hand

give

Move flat O out from chest, as if giving something

(a) **dog**

Snap your fingers, starting with a D, ending with a G

(a) **bone.**

Tap index finger of X on knuckle of left fist

This

Point to an imaginary "this"

old

Zigzag S down from chin, like a long, wavy beard

man  Move thumb of 5 from forehead to chest

came  Point index fingers out, palms up, then flick fingers toward chest

rolling  Circle r's around each other, as if rolling something up

home.  Tap flat O at side of mouth, then at cheekbone

Repeat, substituting the following numbers and words:

two  Hold up index and middle fingers

shoe;  Tap S's, facedown, together twice

three  Hold up thumb and index and middle fingers

knee;  Point to knee

four  Hold up four fingers

door;  Open and close right hand next to left hand

five  Hold up five fingers

hive;  Shape beehive with claw hands

six  Touch tip of thumb to tip of pinky finger, with remaining fingers extended

sticks;  Place right G on top of left G; raise right G up to shape stick

seven  Touch tip of thumb to tip of ring finger, with remaining fingers extended

heaven;  Move flat right hand under left hand, palms down, then move right hand out and up toward "heaven"

eight

Touch tip of thumb to tip of middle finger, with remaining fingers extended

gate

[door];

Open and close right hand next to left hand

nine

Touch tip of thumb to tip of index finger, with remaining fingers extended

spine

[back];

Reach over your shoulder toward your back

ten

Point thumb of A up; wiggle hand side to side

chin.

Point to chin

TEN LITTLE MONKEYS

One  Hold up index finger

little,  Hold out flat hand to show size of a little monkey

two  Hold up index and middle fingers

little,  Hold out flat hand to show size of a little monkey

three  Hold up thumb and index and middle fingers

little  Hold out flat hand to show size of a little monkey

monkeys,  Scratch sides with claw hands like a monkey

four  Hold up four fingers

little,  Hold out flat hand to show size of a little monkey

five  Hold up five fingers

little,  Hold out flat hand to show size of a little monkey

six

Touch tip of thumb to tip of pinky finger, with remaining fingers extended

little

Hold out flat hand to show size of a little monkey

monkeys,

Scratch sides with claw hands like a monkey

seven

Touch tip of thumb to tip of ring finger, with remaining fingers extended

little,  Hold out flat hand to show size of a little monkey

eight  Touch tip of thumb to tip of middle finger, with remaining fingers extended

little,  Hold out flat hand to show size of a little monkey

nine  Touch tip of thumb to tip of index finger, with remaining fingers extended

little  Hold out flat hand to show size of a little monkey

monkeys,  Scratch sides with claw hands like a monkey

ten  Point thumb of A up; wiggle hand side to side

little  Hold out flat hand to show size of a little monkey

monkeys  Scratch sides with claw hands like a monkey

in  Move right fingertips into left O

(the) **zoo!**  Draw Z on left palm

B-I-N-G-O

There

Point to imaginary farmer

(was a) **farmer**

Slide 4 left to right across chin, then add "body" sign, moving open hands down sides of body

had

Place fingertips of cupped hands on chest

(a) **dog,**

Snap your fingers, starting with a D, ending with a G

(and) **Bingo**

Pat leg with B

(was) **his**

Point to imaginary dog

name -o.

Tap right U on top of left U twice, then shape O with fingers and thumb

B  Hold up flat hand, with thumb in middle of palm

I  Extend pinky finger; tuck in remaining fingers and thumb

N  Fold index and middle fingers over thumb; tuck in remaining fingers

G  Extend index finger and thumb, with remaining fingers tucked in, as if in a fist

O!  Shape O with fingers and thumb

B  Hold up flat hand, with thumb in middle of palm

I  Extend pinky finger; tuck in remaining fingers and thumb

N  Fold index and middle fingers over thumb; tuck in remaining fingers

G  Extend index finger and thumb, with remaining fingers tucked in, as if in a fist

O!  Shape O with fingers and thumb

B  Hold up flat hand, with thumb in middle of palm

I  Extend pinky finger; tuck in remaining fingers and thumb

N  Fold index and middle fingers over thumb; tuck in remaining fingers

G  Extend index finger and thumb, with remaining fingers tucked in, as if in a fist

O!  Shape O with fingers and thumb

(and) **Bingo**  Pat leg with B

(was) **his**

Point to imaginary dog

name -o.

Tap right U on top of left U twice, then shape O with fingers and thumb

Repeat song and signs, replacing each letter with a clap, beginning with one clap for B, then two claps for I, then three claps for N, then four claps for G, then five claps for O.

Clap

Clap once

I

Extend pinky finger; tuck in remaining fingers and thumb

N

Fold index and middle fingers over thumb; tuck in remaining fingers

G

Extend index finger and thumb, with remaining fingers tucked in, as if in a fist

O!

Shape O with fingers and thumb

Clap  Clap once

  Extend pinky finger; tuck in remaining fingers and thumb

  Fold index and middle fingers over thumb; tuck in remaining fingers

G  Extend index finger and thumb, with remaining fingers tucked in, as if in a fist

O!  Shape O with fingers and thumb

Clap  Clap once

I  Extend pinky finger; tuck in remaining fingers and thumb

N  Fold index and middle fingers over thumb; tuck in remaining fingers

G  Extend index finger and thumb, with remaining fingers tucked in, as if in a fist

O!  Shape O with fingers and thumb

(and) **Bingo**  Pat leg with B

(was) **his**  Point to imaginary dog

name -o.

Tap right U on top of left U twice, then shape O with fingers and thumb

Repeat, replacing each letter with a clap.

LIONS,
and TIGERS,
and BEARS!
OH MY!

BAA BAA BLACK SHEEP

Baa baa  Move B out from mouth, twice

black  Swipe index finger across forehead

sheep,  Open and close right V while sliding up left arm, as if shearing

have  Place fingertips of cupped hands on chest

you  Point to baby

(any) **wool?**  W slides up left arm

Yes
(sir),  Make S nod up and down

Yes
(sir),

Make S nod up and down

three

Hold up thumb and index and middle fingers

bags

Shape bag with both hands

full.

Brush right flat hand inward over top of left fist

One  Hold up index finger

for  Place right index finger on forehead; rotate finger outward

my  Place flat hand on chest

master
[boss],  Tap right claw on right shoulder

one  Hold up index finger

for  Place right index finger on forehead; rotate finger outward

my  Place flat hand on chest

dame
[woman],  Touch thumb of 5 from chin to chest

and  Move open hand left to right across chest, changing to a flat O

one  Hold up index finger

for  Place right index finger on forehead; rotate finger outward

(the) **little**  Hold out flat hand to show size of child

boy  Pull flat O out from forehead, as if showing the brim of a baseball cap

who  Circle index finger around mouth

lives  Move l's up chest

down  Point down

(the) **lane**
[street].

Zigzag forward both hands, with palms parallel, facing each other

ITSY-BITSY SPIDER

(AKA "EENSY-WEENSY SPIDER")

(The) itsy-
[little]

Hold flat hands apart, palms facing in, fairly close together

bitsy
[littler]

Move hands in closer

spider

Turn claw hands facedown, crossing at the wrists, and wiggle fingers

went

[climbed]

Wiggle two fingers up, as if walking up stairs

up

Point up

(the) **water-**

Tap W on chin

spout.

Shape spout with crooked index finger

Down  Point down

came  Point index fingers out, palms up, then flick fingers toward chest

(the) **rain**  Hold up 5's, then bounce them downward like falling rain

and  Move open hand left to right across chest, changing to a flat O

washed

Touch A's, facing each other, then move them back and forth as if washing

(the) spider

Turn claw hands facedown, crossing at the wrists, and wiggle fingers

out.

Pull right hand out from grasp of left hand

Out came the sun

[sunrise]

Cross forearms; move right C up from left elbow like a rising sun

and  Move open hand left to right across chest, changing to a flat O

dried (up)  Move index finger across chin, changing to an X

all  Move open right hand, palm out, forward and around left hand, landing it palm up in left palm

(the) **rain.**  Hold up 5's, then bounce them down like falling rain

And

Move open hand left to right across chest, changing to a flat O

(the) **itsy-**
[little]

Hold flat hands apart, palms facing in, fairly close together

bitsy
[littler]

Move hands in closer

spider

Turn claw hands facedown, crossing at the wrists, and wiggle fingers

went

[climbed]

Wiggle two fingers up, as if walking up stairs

up

Point up

(the) **spout**

Shape spout with crooked index finger

again.

Cup right hand, palm up, then flip it over so right fingertips land in left palm

OLD MACDONALD HAD A FARM

Old  Zigzag S down from chin, like a long, wavy beard

MacDonald   Change M to D

had  Place fingertips of cupped hands on chest

(a) **farm.**

Slide 4 across chin, left to right

E-

Bend fingers; place bent thumb under fingertips

I-

Extend pinky finger; tuck in remaining fingers and thumb

E-

Bend fingers; place bent thumb under fingertips

I-  Extend pinky finger; tuck in remaining fingers and thumb

O.  Shape O with fingers and thumb

(And) **on**  Place flat right palm on back of flat left hand

(that) **farm**  Slide 4 across chin, left to right

he  Point to imaginary farmer

had  Place fingertips of cupped hands on chest

(a) **cow.**  Place thumb of Y on temple, so pinky finger sticks out like an ear or a horn

E-  Bend fingers; place bent thumb under fingertips

I-  Extend pinky finger; tuck in remaining fingers and thumb

E-  Bend fingers; place bent thumb under fingertips

I-  Extend pinky finger; tuck in remaining fingers and thumb

O.  Shape O with fingers and thumb

With  Place A's together, palms facing each other

(a) **moo moo**  Move M out from mouth, twice

here,  Point down

(and) (a) **moo moo**  Move M out from mouth, twice

there.  Point to imaginary spot

Here  Point down

(a) **moo,**  Move M out from mouth

there  Point to imaginary spot

(a) **moo,**

Move M out from mouth

everywhere

Point index finger up and shake it side to side

(a) **moo moo.**

Move M out from mouth, twice

Old

Zigzag S down from chin, like a long, wavy beard

MacDonald   Change M to D

had  Place fingertips of cupped hands on chest

(a) **farm.**  Slide 4 across chin, left to right

E-  Bend fingers; place bent thumb under fingertips

I-  Extend pinky finger; tuck in remaining fingers and thumb

E-  Bend fingers; place bent thumb under fingertips

I-  Extend pinky finger; tuck in remaining fingers and thumb

O.  Shape O with fingers and thumb

Repeat the song, substituting the following animal and sound signs:

chicken  Open and close thumb and index finger in front of mouth, like a beak

cluck; 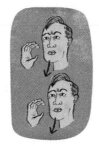 Move C out from mouth

turkey  Shake G down from chin, like a waddle

gobble;  Move G out from mouth

duck  Open and close hand at mouth, like a beak

quack;  Move Q out from mouth

horse  With thumb of U, touch temple, like a horse's ear; bend U down

neigh;  Move N out from mouth

pig  Bend B under chin

oink;  Move O out from mouth

sheep  Open and close right V while sliding up left arm, as if shearing

baa;  Move B out from mouth

dog   Snap your fingers, starting with a D, ending with a G

woof;  Move W out from mouth

cat  Pull thumb and index finger together away from mouth, to show whiskers

meow.  Move M out from mouth

THE BEAR WENT OVER THE MOUNTAIN

(TUNE: "FOR HE'S A JOLLY GOOD FELLOW")

(The) **bear**

Cross arms over chest; scratch at shoulders

(went) **over**

Move right hand, palm facing in, over left hand, palm in

(the) mountain.

Hit top of left fist with right fist, then open both hands up to 5's and move upward, suggesting a mountain slope

(The) bear

Cross arms over chest; scratch at shoulders

(went) over

Move right hand, palm facing in, over left hand, palm in

(the) mountain.

Hit top of left fist with right fist, then open both hands up to 5's and move upward, suggesting a mountain slope

(The) **bear**

Cross arms over chest; scratch at shoulders

(went) **over**

Move right hand, palm facing in, over left hand, palm in

(the) **mountain,**

Hit top of left fist with right fist, then open both hands up to 5's and move upward, suggesting a mountain slope

(to) **see**

Move V out from eyes

what  Strike down left palm with right index fingertip

he  Point to imaginary bear

could

[can]  Move two S's down

see.  Move V out from eyes

(To) **see**

Move V out from eyes

what

Strike down left palm with right index fingertip

he

Point to imaginary bear

could

[can]

Move two S's down

see.  Move V out from eyes

(To) **see**  Move V out from eyes

what  Strike down left palm with right index fingertip

he  Point to imaginary bear

could

[can]

Move two S's down

see.

Move V out from eyes

(The) **other**

Flip palm-down A over to palm up

side

Pass hand down side of body

(of the)
mountain.

Hit top of left fist with right fist, then open both hands up to 5's and move upward, suggesting a mountain slope

(The) **other**

Flip palm-down A over to palm up

side

Pass hand down side of body

(of the)
mountain.

Hit top of left fist with right fist, then open both hands up to 5's and move upward, suggesting a mountain slope

(The) other

Flip palm-down A over to palm up

side

Pass hand down side of body

(of the) mountain,

Hit top of left fist with right fist, then open both hands up to 5's and move upward, suggesting a mountain slope

(was) all

Move open right hand, palm out, forward and around left hand, landing it palm up in left palm

(that) **he**

Point to imaginary bear

could
[can]

Move two S's down

see.

Move V out from eyes

Repeat:

(Was) **all**
(that) **he**
could
see.

(Was) **all**
(that) **he**
could
see.

(The) **other**
side
(of the)
mountain

(was) **all**
(that) **he**
could
see.

HICKORY DICKORY DOCK

Hickory
[letter H]

Extend index and middle fingers, with remaining fingers and thumb tucked in, as if in a fist

dickory
[letter D]

Shape D, with index finger extended, other fingers and thumb touching

dock
[letter D],

Shape D, with index finger extended, other fingers and thumb touching

(the) **mouse**  Brush nose with index finger, right to left

ran

[go]  Point index fingers up, then flip them forward

up  Point up

(the) **clock.**  Tap back of left wrist with right index finger

(The) **clock**  Tap back of left wrist with right index finger

struck  Hit left index finger with right fist

one,  Hold up index finger

(the) **mouse**  Brush nose with index finger, right to left

ran

Point index fingers up, then flip them forward

down,

Point down

hickory

[letter H],

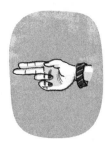

Extend index and middle fingers, with remaining fingers and thumb tucked in, as if in a fist

dickory

[letter D],

Shape D, with index finger extended, other fingers and thumb touching

dock

[letter D].

Shape D, with index finger extended, other fingers and thumb touching

GET UP

and GO!

ACTIVE RHYMES

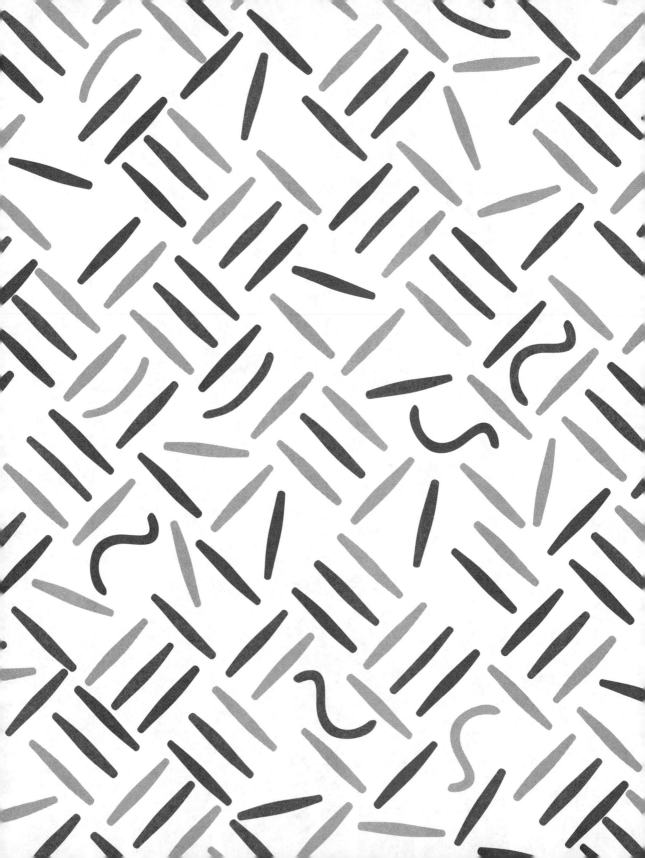

IF YOU'RE HAPPY AND YOU KNOW IT

If

Tap cheek with pinky finger

you('re)

Point to baby

happy

Brush upward on chest with fingertips, alternating hands, twice

and  Move open hand left to right across chest, changing to a flat O

you  Point to baby

know
(it),  Place fingertips of open hand on forehead

clap your hands.  Clap twice

If  Tap cheek with pinky finger

you('re)  Point to baby

happy  Brush upward on chest with fingertips, alternating hands, twice

and  Move open hand left to right across chest, changing to a flat O

you

Point to baby

know

(it),

Place fingertips of open hand on forehead

clap your hands.

Clap twice

If

Tap cheek with pinky finger

you('re)  Point to baby

happy  Brush upward on chest with fingertips, alternating hands, twice

and  Move open hand left to right across chest, changing to a flat O

you  Point to baby

know

(it),

Place fingertips of open hand on forehead

(then) **your**

Hold out palm

face

Circle face with index finger, counterclockwise, beginning at forehead

will

Move flat hand forward from side of head

really  Move index finger forward from chin in a small arch

show  Place right index finger in left palm; move both forward

(it). **If**  Tap cheek with pinky finger

you('re)  Point to baby

happy

Brush upward on chest with fingertips, alternating hands, twice

and

Move open hand left to right across chest, changing to a flat O

you

Point to baby

know
(it),

Place fingertips of open hand on forehead

clap your hands.

Clap twice

Repeat "If you're happy and you know it," replacing "Clap your hands" with the following substitutions:

tap your toe;

Tap toe twice

nod your head;

Nod head twice

pat your tummy.

Pat tummy twice

I'M A LITTLE TEAPOT

I('m)  Point to chest

(a) **little**  Hold flat hands apart, palms facing in, fairly close together

tea-  "Stir" right F inside left O

pot,  Turn down thumb-up Y as if pouring from a teapot

short  Show height with flat hand, palm down

and  Move open hand left to right across chest, changing to a flat O

stout.  Shapes L's facing each other, then move them apart, to show large size

Here  Point down

(is) **my**  Place flat hand on chest

handle,  Place hand on hip to form handle

here  Point down

(is) **my**  Place flat hand on chest

spout.  Hold other arm out straight to form spout

When  Touch right index fingertip to left index fingertip; circle right index finger forward and back around

I  Point to chest

get

[become]

Cross palms together, right on top of left; twist hands around

all

Move open right hand, palm up, forward and around left hand, landing it palm up in left palm

steamed

[warm]

Shape flat O at mouth, then open it up and out to a claw, as if exhaling warm breath

up,

Point up

hear  Point to ear

me  Point to chest

shout.  Cup hand at mouth; move up and out to a claw

(Just) **tip**  Lean over and tip arm like a spout

me  Point to chest

(over) **and**  Move open hand left to right across chest, changing to a flat O

pour  Turn down thumbs-up Y as if pouring from a teapot

me  Point to chest

out!

Pull right hand out from grasp of left hand

LONDON BRIDGE

London

Circle L near side of head

Bridge

Hold left arm flat, place right V under left wrist, and move V to under elbow

(is) **falling down,**

Flip palm-down right V into left palm so it lands palm up

falling down,

Flip palm-down right V into left palm so it lands palm up

falling down.

Flip palm-down right V into left palm so it lands palm up

London

Circle L near side of head

Bridge

Hold left arm flat, place right V under left wrist, and move V to under elbow

(is) **falling down,**

Flip palm-down right V into left palm so it lands palm up

my

Place flat hand on chest

fair
[good]

Touch mouth with right fingertips, then move down and land it palm up in left palm

lady!

Move A from side of chin down to open hand at chest

RING-AROUND-THE-ROSY

Ring around

Circle right index finger, pointing down, around left flat O, pointing up

(the) **rosy** [red].

Swipe index finger down from lip

(A) **pocket**

Tuck right fingers into left O

full

Brush right flat hand inward over top of left fist

(of) **posies**
[flowers].

Tap right side of cheek, then left side of cheek with flat O, as if passing a flower under your nose

Ashes,

Hold up flat O's, then brush thumbs against fingertips, as if feeling grit/ashes

ashes,

Hold up flat O's, then brush thumbs against fingertips, as if feeling grit/ashes

we

With index finger, touch right shoulder, then left shoulder

all

Move open right hand, palm out, forward and around left hand, landing it palm up in left palm

fall down!

Flip palm-down right V into left palm so it lands palm up

JACK AND JILL

Jack  Sign J by forehead

and  Move open hand left to right across chest, changing to a flat O

Jill  Sign J by chin

went

[go]

Point index fingers up, then
flip them forward

up

Point up

(the) **hill**

Hit top of left fist with right fist,
then open both hands up to 5's
and move upward, suggesting
a hill slope

(to) **fetch**

[get]

Place right claw hand facing
left above left claw hand facing
right, then pull both hands
toward chest while closing
hands to fists

(a) **pail**
[bucket]

Hold fist down at side, then pull it up, as if pulling up a bucket

(of) **water.**

Tap W on chin

Jack

Sign J by forehead

fell down

Flip palm-down right V into left palm so it lands palm up

and

Move open hand left to right across chest, changing to a flat O

broke

Bring sides of both fists together, then "break" them apart

his

Point to imaginary Jack

crown

[head],

Touch top of head with fingertips, then touch bottom of chin

and

Move open hand left to right across chest, changing to a flat O

Jill

Sign J by chin

came

Point index fingers out, palms up, then flick fingers toward chest

tumbling

[falling]

Flip palm-down right V into left palm so it lands palm up

after.

Cup left hand with right hand;
move right hand out

SURPRISE! SURPRISE!

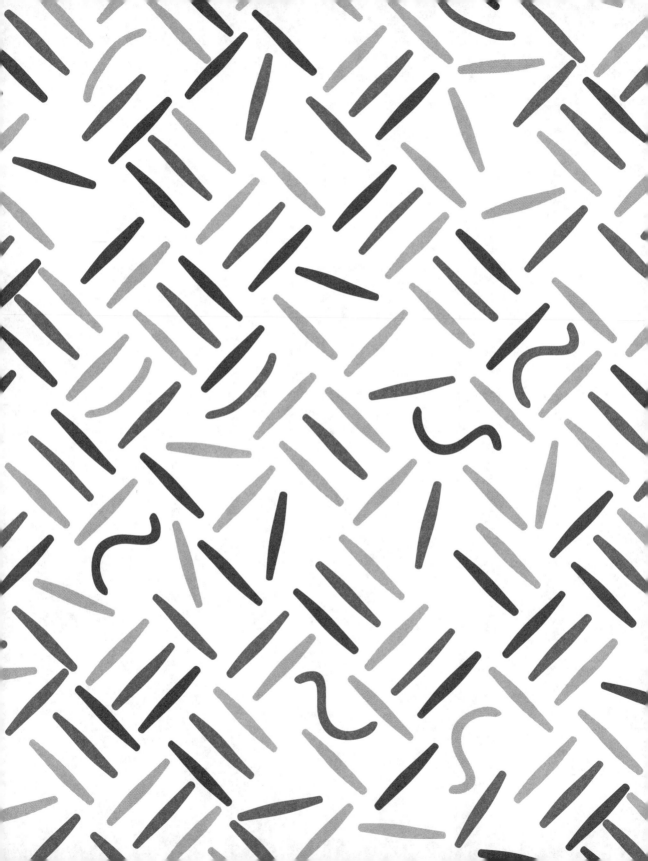

PAT-A-CAKE

Pat   Clap twice

(-a-) **cake,**  Touch right claw to left palm twice, as if showing a cake on a platter

pat   Clap twice

(-a-) **cake,**

Touch right claw to left palm twice, as if showing a cake on a platter

baker('s)

Pat left palm with right hand once, then flip right hand over and land it palm up in left palm, as if flipping a pancake

man,

Move thumb of 5 from forehead to chest

bake

Pat left palm with right hand once, then flip right hand over and land it palm up in left palm, as if flipping a pancake

us  Touch right shoulder, then left shoulder with index finger

(a) **cake**  Touch right claw to left palm twice, as if showing a cake on a platter

(as) **fast**  Shape L's, point them out, then pull them in toward your chest and change them into X's

(as) **you**  Point to imaginary baker

can.

Move two S's down

Roll

Circle R's around each other, as if rolling something up

it

Point to imaginary cake

and

Move open hand left to right across chest, changing to a flat O

pat   Clap twice

it  Point to imaginary cake

and  Move open hand left to right across chest, changing to a flat O

mark  "Write" on left palm with right X

it  Point to imaginary cake

with  Place A's together, palms facing each other

(a) **B,**  Hold up flat hand, with thumb in middle of palm

(and) **throw**  Move flat O's forward from chest as hands open up

(it) **in**

Move right fingertips into left O

(the) **oven**

Move right O forward under left flat hand, palm down

for

Place right index finger on forehead; rotate finger outward

baby

Put arms together and rock an imaginary baby

and  Move open hand left to right across chest, changing to a flat O

me.  Point to chest

WHERE IS THUMBKIN?

Where

Point index finger up; move it side to side

(is)
thumbkin?

Hold up thumb and wiggle it

Where

Point index finger up; move it side to side

(is)
thumbkin?

Hold up thumb and wiggle it

Here

Point down

I

Point to chest

(am.)

Hold up other thumb and wiggle it

Here  Point down

I  Point to chest

(am.)  Hold up other thumb and wiggle it

How  Hold fingers of cupped hands together, palms down, then turn hands palm up

(are) **you**

Point to baby

(this)
morning?

Place left hand in crook of right arm; raise right hand, palm up, as if sun is rising

Very

Shape L's facing each other, then move them apart

well
[good],

Touch mouth with right fingertips, then move right hand down and land it palm up in left palm

I  Point to chest

thank  Touch mouth with fingertips, then move them out

you.  Point to baby

Run  Link right index finger and left thumb; move fingers forward

away.  Flip hand out, indicating "go away"

Run  Link right index finger and left thumb; move fingers forward

away.  Flip hand out, indicating "go away"

Repeat, substituting the following fingers and signs:

Where

Point index finger up; move it side to side

(is)

pointer?

Wiggle index finger

Where

Point index finger up; move it side to side

(is) **tall man?**

Wiggle middle finger

Where

Point index finger up; move it side to side

(is)

ring man?

Wiggle ring finger

Where

Point index finger up; move it side to side

(is) **baby?**

Wiggle pinky finger

Where

Point index finger up; move it side to side

(is the)
family?

Place circles of two F's together; move out and around until pinky fingers touch

POP GOES
THE WEASEL

Round

Circle right index finger, pointing down, around left flat O, pointing up

and

Move open hand left to right across chest, changing to flat O

round

Circle right index finger, pointing down, around left flat O, pointing up

(the)
cobbler's
[shoe]

Tap S's, facedown, together twice

bench
[table],

Hold arms parallel, right over left, and tap together twice

(the)
monkey

Scratch sides with claw hands like a monkey

chased

Move fists to your sides, as if you're about to give chase

(the)

weasel.

Brush nose with W, right to left

(The)

monkey

Scratch sides with claw hands
like a monkey

thought

[think]

Point to forehead with
index finger

it

Point to the imaginary scene

(was) **all**

Move open right hand, palm out, forward and around left hand, landing it palm up in left palm

(in) **fun.**

With right U, touch nose, then move right U down to land on left U

Pop!

Tuck right F inside left O, then change right F to flat hand on top of left O

goes

Point index fingers up; flip fingers forward

(the)

weasel.

Brush nose with W, right to left

THIS LITTLE PIGGY

This

Point to big toe

little

Hold flat hands apart, palms
facing in, fairly close together

piggy

Bend B under chin

went

[go]

Point index fingers up, then flip them forward

(to) **market**

[store].

Move flat O's back and forth, twice

This

Point to second toe

little

Hold flat hands apart, palms facing in, fairly close together

piggy  Bend B under chin

stayed  Move palm-down Y downward

home.  Tap flat O at side of mouth, then at cheekbone

This  Point to third toe

little

Hold flat hands apart, palms facing in, fairly close together

piggy

Bend B under chin

had

[have]

Place fingertips of cupped hands on chest

roast beef

[meat].

With right thumb and index finger, pinch left hand in between thumb and index finger

This  Point to fourth toe

little  Hold flat hands apart, palms facing in, fairly close together

piggy  Bend B under chin

had
[have]  Place fingertips of cupped hands on chest

none.  Move flat O's forward

This  Point to pinky toe

little  Hold flat hands apart, palms facing in, fairly close together

piggy  Bend B under chin

cried

Brush index fingers down cheeks, alternating, as if tears are running down

"wee, wee, wee"

Move E's out from side of mouth simultaneously, three times

all

Move open right hand, palm out, forward and around left hand, landing it palm up in left palm

(the) **way**

Move flat hands, palms facing in, forward, making the shape of a road or path

home.

Tap flat O at side of mouth, then at cheekbone

BABY BUMBLEBEE

I('m)  Point to chest

bring(ing)  Hold hands in front of you, palms up, then move them to the side

home  Tap flat O at side of mouth, then at cheekbone

(a) **baby**

Put arms together and rock an imaginary baby

bumblebee

[bee].

Tap cheek with F, then swipe down cheek with open hand as if you've just been stung and you're swatting the bee away

Won't

[will]

Move flat hand forward from side of head

my

Place flat hand on chest

mommy

Tap thumb of open hand on chin twice

be

[feel]

Touch middle finger to chest; move finger up

(so) **proud**

With thumb of fist, touch chest; move thumb up

(of) **me.**

Point to chest

I('m)  Point to chest

bring(ing)  Hold hands in front of you, palms up, then move them to the side

home  Tap flat O at side of mouth, then at cheekbone

(a) **baby**  Put arms together and rock an imaginary baby

bumblebee

[bee].

Tap cheek with F, then swipe down cheek with open hand as if you've just been stung and you're swatting the bee away

Ouch!

React to sting

It

Point to imaginary bee

stung

Tap back of hand sharply with crooked index finger

me!

Point to chest

HUSH-A-BYE and NIGHTY NIGHT

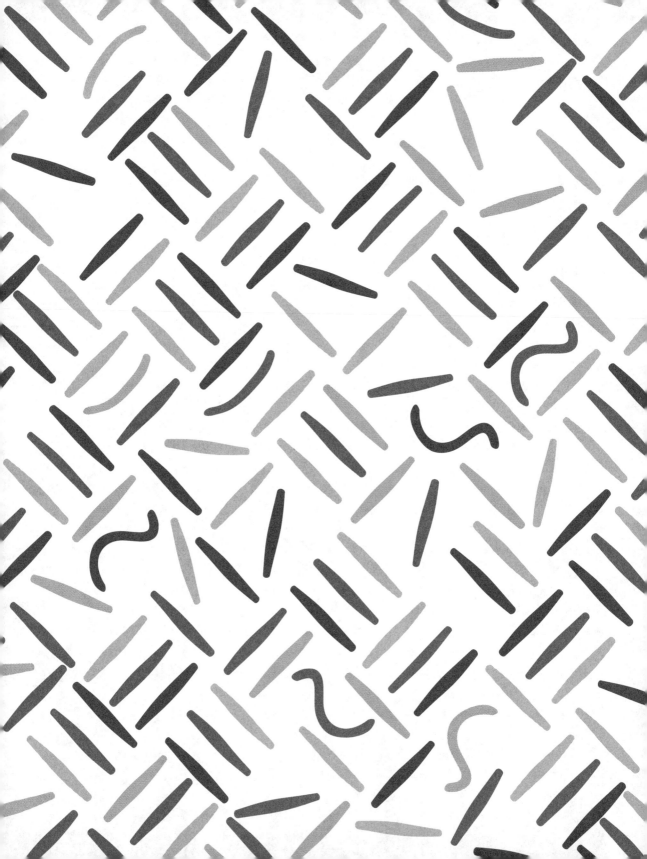

ROCK-A-BYE BABY

Rock-a-bye baby

[rock],

Put arms together and rock an imaginary baby

in

Move right fingertips into left O

(the) **treetop**

[tree].

Hold right arm up to make a tree, with elbow resting on back of left hand

When

Touch right index fingertip to left index fingertip; circle right index finger forward and back around

(the) **wind (blows),**

Move open hands, facing each other, back and forth like wind blowing

(the) **cradle**

[bed]

Place palms together; rest hands on side of face

will

Move flat hand forward from side of head

rock.  Put arms together and rock an imaginary baby

When  Touch right index fingertip to left index fingertip; circle right index finger forward and back around

(the) **bough**

[tree]  Hold right arm up to make a tree, with elbow resting on back of left hand

breaks,  Bring sides of both fists together, then "break" them apart

(the) cradle
[bed]

Place palms together; rest hands on side of face

will

Move flat hand forward from side of head

fall,

Flip palm-down right V into left palm so it lands palm up

(and) down

Point down

will

Move flat hand forward from side of head

come

[go]

Point index fingers up, then flick them forward

baby,

Put arms together and rock an imaginary baby

cradle

[bed]

Place palms together; rest hands on side of face

and

Move open hand left to right across chest, changing to a flat O

all.

Move open right hand, palm out, forward and around left hand, landing it palm up in left palm

ARE YOU SLEEPING?

(Are) **you**  Point to baby

sleeping?  Place open hand on forehead; close to flat O at chin

(Are) **you**  Point to baby

sleeping,  Place open hand on forehead; close to flat O at chin

baby  Put arms together and rock an imaginary baby

boy  Pull flat O out from forehead, as if showing the brim of a baseball cap

[girl for girl baby]  Move thumb of A down from cheek to chin

baby  Put arms together and rock an imaginary baby

boy  Pull flat O out from forehead, as if showing the brim of a baseball cap

[girl for girl baby]  Move thumb of A down from cheek to chin

Morning  Place left hand in crook of right arm; raise right hand, palm up, as if sun is rising

bells are ring(ing).

With side of right Q, hit left palm, as if the clapper is hitting the bell; then wiggle Q to the right, as if the sound is reverberating

Morning

Place left hand in crook of right arm; raise right hand, palm up, as if sun is rising

bells are ring(ing).

With side of right Q, hit left palm, as if the clapper is hitting the bell; then wiggle Q to the right, as if the sound is reverberating

Ding, dong, ding,

Repeat sign of "bells are ringing"

Ding, dong, ding.

Repeat sign of "bells are ringing"

HUSH, LITTLE BABY

Hush

[quiet],

Place index finger at lips as if shushing someone

little

Hold out flat hand to show size of a little baby

baby,

Put arms together and rock an imaginary baby

don't  Hold thumb extended from fist under chin; move arm out

say  Move index finger forward from mouth

(a) **word.**  Tap right thumb and index finger on extended left index finger

Mama('s)  Tap chin with open hand

go(ing)

Point index fingers up, then flip them forward

(to) **buy**

Place right flat O in palm of flat left hand, then move O forward, as if paying money

you

Point to baby

(a) **mocking-**

[copy]

Place right open hand in left palm; close to flat O

bird.

Open and close index finger and thumb at side of mouth, like a beak

Hush

[quiet],

Place index finger at lips as if shushing someone

little

Hold out flat hand to show size of a little baby

baby,

Put arms together and rock an imaginary baby

don't  Hold thumb extended from fist under chin; move arm out

you  Point to baby

cry.  Brush index fingers down cheeks, alternating, as if tears are running down

Daddy  Tap forehead twice with thumb of open hand

love(s)  Cross arms over chest, with hands in fists

you,  Point to baby

and  Move open hand left to right across chest, changing to a flat O

so do

[also]  Point index fingers out; tap fingers once to the left, once to the right

I.  Point to chest

TWINKLE, TWINKLE LITTLE STAR

Twinkle,  Open and close G at side of eye

twinkle  Open and close G at side of eye

little  Hold flat hands apart, palms facing in, fairly close together

star,  Point index fingers up, then brush them back and forth against each other

how  Hold fingers of cupped hands together, palms down, then turn hands palm up

  Point to chest

wonder  Circle index finger at side of forehead

what

Strike down left palm with right index fingertip

you

Point up at imaginary star

are.

With palms up, shrug

Up

Point up

above  Rest right hand, palm down, on top of left hand, palm down; right hand circles upward

(the) **world**  Place right W on top of left W, circle right W forward and around, then place it back on top of left W

(so) **high,**  Move H up

like  Move Y palm-down from left to right

(a) **diamond**

Tap right D ring finger on back of left hand

in

Move right fingertips into left O

(the) **sky.**

Sweep hand, palm down, overhead from left to right, indicating the sky

Twinkle,

Open and close G at side of eye

twinkle,  Open and close G at side of eye

little  Hold flat hands apart, palms facing in, fairly close together

star,  Point index fingers up, then brush them back and forth against each other

how  Hold fingers of cupped hands together, palms down, then turn hands palm up

I — Point to chest

wonder — Circle index finger at side of forehead

what — Strike down left palm with right index fingertip

you — Point up at imaginary star

are.  With palms up, shrug

NOW I LAY ME DOWN TO SLEEP

Now  Cup hands, palm up, then move them down

I  Point to chest

lay  Lay faceup right V on left palm

me  Point to chest

down  Point down

(to) **sleep.**  Place open hand on forehead; close to a flat O at chin

 I  Point to chest

pray

Place palms together; move them back and forth

(the) **Lord**

Pull right flat hand, palm facing left, back in an arch

my

Place flat hand on chest

soul

Place right F on top of left F; pull F's apart

(to) **keep.**

Tap right K on top of left K

Guard

Cross wrists with hands in fists; move both fists forward

me

Point to chest

while

Point index fingers out; move them forward

Point to chest

sleep

Place open hand on forehead; close to a flat O at chin

tonight,

Rest right cupped hand, palm down, on top of left hand, palm down

and

Move open hand left to right across chest, changing to a flat O

wake  Shape closed G's at side of eyes, then move them apart as if eyes are opening

me  Point to chest

safe  Cross S's at wrist, face in, then uncross them and turn them face out

(at) **dawn's**
[morning]  Place left hand in crook of right arm; raise right hand, palm up, as if sun is rising

first  Touch right index finger to left thumb, as if counting

light.  Hold flat O's overhead, then open them to 5's, as if light rays are shining down

CELEBRATE!

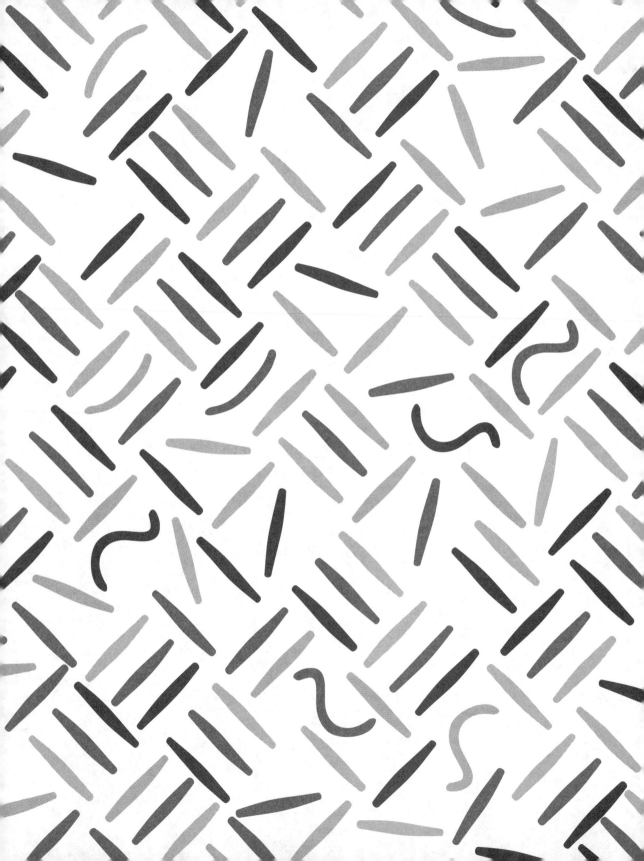

HAPPY
BIRTHDAY

Happy

Brush upward on chest with fingertips, alternating hands, twice

birthday

Touch middle finger to bottom lip, then to chest

(to) **you.**

Point to baby

Happy

Brush upward on chest with fingertips, alternating hands, twice

birthday

Touch middle finger to bottom lip, then to chest

(to) **you.**

Point to baby

Happy

Brush upward on chest with fingertips, alternating hands, twice

birthday,

Touch middle finger to bottom lip, then to chest

dear

[love]

Cross arms over chest, with hands in fists

[person's

name].

Use person's name sign (see page 7 of the introduction for explanation)

Happy

Brush upward on chest with fingertips, alternating hands, twice

birthday  Touch middle finger to bottom lip, then to chest

(to) **you.**  Point to baby

YANKEE DOODLE DANDY

Yankee  Wiggle Y

Doodle  Wiggle D

went  Point index fingers up, then flip them forward

(to) **town,**

Join fingertips to form the roof of a house; repeat, moving to the right

riding

Place right V upside down on side of left hand

on

Place flat right palm on back of flat left hand

(a) **pony.**

With thumb of U, touch temple, like a horse's ear; bend U down

Stuck  Move V to side of neck, as if sticking in throat

(a) **feather**  Arc F up from back of head

in  Move right fingertips into left O

(his) **cap**  Touch top of head with flat hand

(and) called

[named]

Tap right U on top of left U, twice

it

Point to imaginary cap

macaroni.

Shape two M's, side by side; wiggle them and move them out to sides

WE WISH YOU A MERRY CHRISTMAS

We

With index finger, touch right shoulder, then left shoulder

wish

Move C, palm in, down chest

you

Point to baby

(a) **merry**
[happy]

Brush upward on chest with fingertips, alternating hands, twice

Christmas,

Move faces-out C, left to right in front of face

we

With index finger, touch right shoulder, then left shoulder

wish

Move C, palm in, down chest

you

Point to baby

(a) **merry**

[happy]

Brush upward on chest with fingertips, alternating hands, twice

Christmas,

Move faces-out C, left to right in front of face

we

With index finger, touch right shoulder, then left shoulder

wish  Move C, palm in, down chest

you  Point to baby

(a) **merry**
[happy]  Brush upward on chest with fingertips, alternating hands, twice

Christmas,  Move faces-out C, left to right in front of face

and  Move open hand left to right across chest, changing to a flat O

(a) **happy**  Brush upward on chest with fingertips, alternating hands, twice

new  Brush right cupped hand, palm up, right to left inside left flat hand, palm up

year.  Place right fist on top of left fist, circle right fist forward and around, then place it back on top of left fist

JINGLE BELLS

Jingle bells,

Hit left palm with side of right Q, as if hitting a bell, three times (one for each syllable)

jingle bells,

Hit left palm with side of right Q, as if hitting a bell, three times (one for each syllable)

jingle

Hit left palm with side of right Q, as if hitting a bell; then wiggle Q to the right, as if the bell is reverberating

all  Move open right hand, palm out, forward and around left hand, landing it palm up in left palm

(the) **way.**  Move flat hands, palms facing in, forward, making the shape of a road or path

Oh,  Shape O with fingers and thumb

what  Strike down left palm with right index fingertip

fun  With right U, touch nose, then move right U down to land on left U

it  Point to the side

(is to) **ride**  Place right V upside down on side of left hand

in  Move right fingertips into left O

(a) **one-**  Hold up index finger

horse  With thumb of U, touch temple, like a horse's ear; bend U down

open  Place sides of hands together, palms out, then open hands up like doors, with palms facing each other

sleigh!  Point index fingers toward chest, arc them out and down, palms up, then pull them in toward chest, as if shaping the blades of a sleigh

DREIDEL SONG

I

Point to chest

have

Place fingertips of cupped hands on chest

(a) **little**

Hold flat hands apart, palms facing in, fairly close together

dreidel.  Point right index finger down and left index finger up; rotate fingers around each other

I  Point to chest

made  Place right fist on top of left fist; twist both fists

it  Point to imaginary dreidel

out

Pull right hand out from grasp of left hand

(of) **clay.**

With cupped hands, palms facing each other, squeeze "clay"

When

Touch right index fingertip to left index fingertip; circle right index finger forward and back around

it('s)

Point to imaginary dreidel

dry  Move index finger across chin, changing to an X

and  Move open hand left to right across chest, changing to a flat O

ready,  Point facedown R's to one side, then move them to other side in unison

(then)
dreidel  Point right index finger down and left index finger up; rotate fingers around each other

I  Point to chest

shall  Move flat hand forward from side of head

play.  Twist Y's back and forth

RESOURCES

Don't stop now! Keep those fingers moving by checking out some of the following sign language resources.

Books

Learn to Sign the Fun Way!, by Penny Warner (Three Rivers Press)
Filled with signs for vocabulary words that kids use the most, this book also offers dozens of games to play using ASL.

Signing Fun, by Penny Warner (Gallaudet University Press)
More signs and signing games for kids eight to fourteen (and their teachers and parents too!).

Baby Sign Language Basics: Early Communication for Hearing Babies and Toddlers, by Monta Briant (Hay House)
Learn basic signs to use with your baby.

My First Animal Signs, by Anthony Lewis (Child's Play International)
Teach your baby signs she'll love—all about animals.

Baby's Favorite Places (Baby Einstein)
Broaden your baby's vocabulary with signs for familiar places.

Videos

How to Sign with Your Baby, by Smart Hands

Watch and learn basic signs to use with your baby.

My Baby Can Talk, by Baby Hands Productions

More basic vocabulary words for parents and babies.

My First Signs, by Marlee Matlin (Baby Einstein)

The Academy Award–winning actress demonstrates simple signs for baby.

Signing Time, Volumes 1–12, by Two Little Hands Productions

A collection of signs you can use with your baby, divided into categories.

Your Baby Can Talk, by Your Baby Can Talk, Inc.

Another video of basic signs.

Games and Activities
(available online from HarrisComm.com or at many educational supply stores)

The American Sign Language Handshape Puzzle Book,

by Betty Miller

Fill out the puzzle book for finger spelling practice.

Sign It!

A board game that challenges you to sign ASL vocabulary words
on flash cards.

Keep Quiet!

A sign language Boggle-type game; roll the dice and form words
using manual alphabet letters.

ASLingo

Just like bingo, only with sign vocabulary.

See It and Sign It

A multilevel game that teaches signs in six word categories
and comes with a DVD.

Finger Alphabet Lotto

A matching game for learning the sign language alphabet.

Sign language playing cards

Play your favorite games—in sign!

Flash cards for learning sign language

For basic practice in learning to sign.

Vocabulary Web Sites

ASLPro.com

This is a great site for finding vocabulary words that have been
translated into ASL. Free and easy to access.

CommTechLab.msu.edu/sites/aslweb/browser.htm

Another great sign language dictionary site.

Lifeprint.com

More signs presented in short video clips.

HandSpeak.com

Another good resource for all things ASL.

Baby Sign Language Class Finder
(for the United States)

Babies-and-sign-language.com/parent-baby-signing-classes.html

Internet Sign Games

- SurfnetKids.com—Finger-spelling concentration
- Funbrain.com—Alphabet/number game
- EnchantedLearning.com—Flash cards
- Apples4theTeacher.com—Finger-spelling game

ACKNOWLEDGMENTS

Many thanks to James Andrews, Dr. Linda Barde, Neil Christiansen, Peggy Garvin, Dr. Eileen Jackson, Jamie Miller, Stan Ruppert, Dr. Arthurlene Towner, Ivey Wallace, and Beverly Wilson for their inspiration, guidance, and support.

A special thanks to Lindsay Orman and Emily Timberlake, my wonderful editors; Gilbert Ford, a gifted illustrator; and Lilly Ghahremani and Stefanie Von Borstel, my extraordinary agents.

INDEX

About the Author

Penny Warner has a bachelor's degree in child development and a master's degree in special education/deafness. She's taught deaf infants and children, as well as American Sign Language to hearing and deaf people for two decades, and she currently teaches child development at Diablo Valley College. She's published three books on infant development and two children's sign language books, *Learn to Sign the Fun Way!* and *Signing Fun*. Her books have won national awards, garnered excellent reviews, and been printed in fourteen countries. Warner lives in Danville, California, and has two children and four grandchildren.

About the Illustrator

Gilbert Ford was born in Jackson, Mississippi, into a family of professional photographers. Instead of picking up a camera and joining the family business, he moved to Brooklyn, New York, to pursue a career in illustration. Some of his clients have been the *New York Times*, the *Wall Street Journal*, *Forbes*, the *Atlantic Monthly*, Little, Brown, Harcourt, Disney/Hyperion, Chronicle Books, Sterling, Target, Blue Note, and NPR. He is also the author/illustrator of the picture book *Flying Lessons*.